Cozy Christmas: A Mindfulness Christmas Coloring Book for Adults

Festive Scenes and Winter Mindfulness Activities for Relaxation, Meditation, and Stress Relief

Beatrice Winters

Foreword

The holiday season brings with it a blend of joy, wonder, and, at times, the stress of busyness and expectations. It's a time when we can find ourselves caught between the warmth of cherished traditions and the hustle of seasonal commitments.

This Mindfulness Christmas Coloring Book was created as a sanctuary for you—a place to pause, unwind, and reconnect with the magic of the season through the simple, meditative act of coloring.

Coloring is more than an artistic expression; it's a gentle reminder to stay present. When we take the time to fill a page with color, we slow our minds, engage our senses, and let go of the pressures that pull at us. Each page in this book has been thoughtfully designed to invite you into moments of peace and reflection, from intricate mandalas that echo the quiet beauty of snowflakes to cozy holiday scenes that evoke warmth and comfort.

You'll also find moments of mindfulness woven throughout these pages, such as guided breathing exercises, mantras, and journal prompts, all included to help deepen your relaxation and bring awareness to the present. Whether you're coloring by the light of the Christmas tree, sipping on a warm cup of cocoa, or taking a mindful break from your day, let each page be a reminder to savor the small joys of the season.

As you turn the pages and let your creativity flow, may you find moments of stillness and joy, and may each color you choose be a step towards inner calm. This holiday season, take this opportunity to nurture yourself, appreciate the present, and let the spirit of mindfulness fill your heart.

Happy coloring, and may peace and warmth be with you.

With gratitude and festive wishes,

Beatrice Winters

What Does Other Colorers Say

Review Quotes

"Absolutely Perfect for Relaxation!"

"I've tried many adult coloring books, but this one is exceptional. The combination of festive scenes, mindful breathing exercises, and positive affirmations has turned my holiday downtime into true moments of peace. Highly recommend it for anyone looking to unwind during the busy season." Emily R., London, UK

"Beautiful Designs with an Extra Touch of Mindfulness"

"The mindful coloring guide and affirmations throughout the pages make this book stand out. I feel more relaxed and centered after each session. A wonderful way to celebrate the season while practicing self-care." Sofia P., Toronto, Canada

"A True Seasonal Treat"

"The Cozy Christmas Mindfulness Coloring Book exceeded my expectations. The winter scenes are intricate and soothing, and the breathing exercises were a thoughtful addition. I found myself looking forward to these mindful moments every day." Liam K., Dublin, Ireland

"A Must-Have for the Holidays"

"I bought this as a gift for myself, and it was the best decision! The combination of coloring, affirmations, and mindful tips has helped me de-stress and enjoy the holiday season more fully. This book is a gem." Aisha M., Cape Town, South Africa

"Perfect for a Mindful Holiday Season"

"Each page of this book is filled with beauty and intention. The guided breathing exercises make it easy to center myself before coloring. It's a wonderful way to slow down, relax, and enjoy the holidays with a mindful touch." Miguel R., Madrid, Spain

TIPS FOR MINDFUL COLORING

Coloring mindfully is more than just filling in shapes—it's an opportunity to slow down, focus, and immerse yourself in the present moment. Here are some practical tips on how to practice mindful coloring:

1. Create a Calm Environment
    •Tip: "Set up your coloring space in a quiet, comfortable area. Dim the lights slightly or add a soft lamp, and play gentle background music if it helps you relax. This sets the stage for a peaceful coloring session."

2. Take a Deep Breath
    •Tip: "Before you start, take a moment to close your eyes and take a deep breath. Breathe in for four counts, hold for a moment, and exhale slowly. Let go of any stress or tension and prepare to focus on the colors and patterns in front of you."

3. Choose Colors That Speak to You
    •Tip: "Select colors that resonate with how you feel or how you'd like to feel. Don't overthink your choices; let your intuition guide you. If you're seeking calm, opt for cool tones. For a boost of energy, choose warm, vibrant colors."

4. Focus on Each Stroke
    •Tip: "As you color, pay attention to the movement of your pencil or marker. Notice how the color flows onto the page, the texture of the paper, and the sound as you fill in the spaces. This helps anchor you in the present moment."
    —to infuse your coloring with a cozy warmth and positivity. Orange is perfect for hearth scenes, decorative ribbons, and holiday treats, bringing a sense of comfort and cheer."

5. Let Go of Perfection
    •Tip: "Mindful coloring is about the process, not the end result. Release any pressure to make your page look 'perfect.' Enjoy the freedom of creative expression and remember, there are no mistakes—only unique touches."

6. Pause Between Sections
    •Tip: "When you finish a part of the design, pause to appreciate your progress. Take a deep breath and admire the colors and patterns you've brought to life before moving on to the next section."

7. Engage Your Senses
    •Tip: "Bring your senses into the experience by noticing the feel of the pencil in your hand, the scent of any candles or essential oils in the room, and the visual delight of the colors on the page."

8. Be Present with Your Thoughts
   • Tip: "As you color, thoughts may come and go. Acknowledge them without judgment, and gently bring your attention back to the coloring. This helps you practice being present and aware."

9. Embrace Your Emotions
   • Tip: "If you're feeling a strong emotion, use your coloring as a way to channel and process it. Choose colors that reflect how you feel—whether that's soft blues for calm or bright yellows for joy."

10. Reflect When Finished
    • Tip: "Once you complete a coloring session, take a moment to reflect on how you feel. Did the activity bring you relaxation or joy? Carry this sense of mindfulness with you as you go about your day."

Bonus Tip: Consider pairing your coloring session with mindful practices like repeating a mantra, sipping a warm drink slowly, or doing a brief meditation beforehand to deepen the relaxation.

These tips can be included at the beginning of your book as a "Mindful Coloring Guide" or sprinkled throughout as reminders on different pages to help readers stay engaged in a mindful practice

USING SPECIFIC COLORS

Here are guided coloring tips that suggest using specific colors to evoke certain feelings, enhancing the mindful experience while coloring this Mindfulness Christmas Coloring Book:

1. Blue for Calm and Serenity
    - Guided Tip: "Incorporate shades of blue—such as sky blue, turquoise, or navy—into your coloring to evoke a sense of calm and tranquility. Use blue when coloring backgrounds, snowy scenes, or peaceful winter skies to help soothe your mind and invite relaxation."

2. Green for Renewal and Balance
    - Guided Tip: "Use soft greens and deep forest hues to bring a sense of renewal and balance to your coloring. Green is perfect for trees, holly leaves, and nature-inspired designs. Let this color remind you of growth and fresh starts, even in the stillness of winter."

3. Red for Warmth and Energy
    - Guided Tip: "Introduce reds—from bright cherry to deep burgundy—when you want to add warmth and energy to your artwork. Red can be used in festive elements like ornaments, poinsettias, or cozy fireside scenes, sparking joy and vibrancy on the page."

4. White and Silver for Purity and Clarity
    - Guided Tip: "Use white spaces intentionally or add silver highlights to symbolize purity, clarity, and lightness. These colors are ideal for creating contrast and adding a touch of elegance to snowflakes, frosty details, and winter wonderlands."

5. Gold for Joy and Celebration
    - Guided Tip: "Bring touches of gold into your coloring to evoke feelings of joy, celebration, and abundance. Whether it's holiday bells, stars, or candlelight, gold accents can add a festive, uplifting touch that reflects the season's warmth."

6. Purple for Imagination and Magic
    - Guided Tip: "Choose purple hues—like lavender and royal purple—to introduce a sense of magic and creativity. This color is perfect for mystical winter elements, starry night scenes, or whimsical decorations, sparking wonder and inspiration."

7. Brown for Comfort and Grounding
    - Guided Tip: "Use shades of brown, from light taupe to rich chocolate, to evoke a sense of comfort and grounding. Browns can be used for log cabins, warm cocoa mugs, and cozy wooden details, creating a homey, inviting atmosphere."

8. Yellow for Happiness and Light
　•Guided Tip: "Add yellow touches to bring light, hope, and cheerfulness to your art. Soft yellows can represent candle glow or twinkling holiday lights, while brighter yellows can highlight sunlit elements and evoke feelings of joy."

9. Pink for Love and Compassion
　•Guided Tip: "Integrate pinks into your designs to express love, kindness, and compassion. Whether it's soft blush or vibrant magenta, pink adds warmth and a personal touch to holiday scenes, hearts, and thoughtful details."

10. Orange for Warmth and Positivity
　•Guided Tip: "Use shades of orange—like pumpkin and amber—to infuse your coloring with a cozy warmth and positivity. Orange is perfect for hearth scenes, decorative ribbons, and holiday treats, bringing a sense of comfort and cheer."

A GUIDED BREATHING EXCERSIZE

The stillness of winter brings clarity and balance.

Tips for Effective Breathing:

- Focus on making your exhale longer than your inhale. This helps signal your parasympathetic nervous system to promote relaxation.
- Keep your breaths smooth and gentle. Avoid straining or pushing beyond your comfort level.
- As you breathe, imagine the tension melting away and being replaced with calmness and warmth.

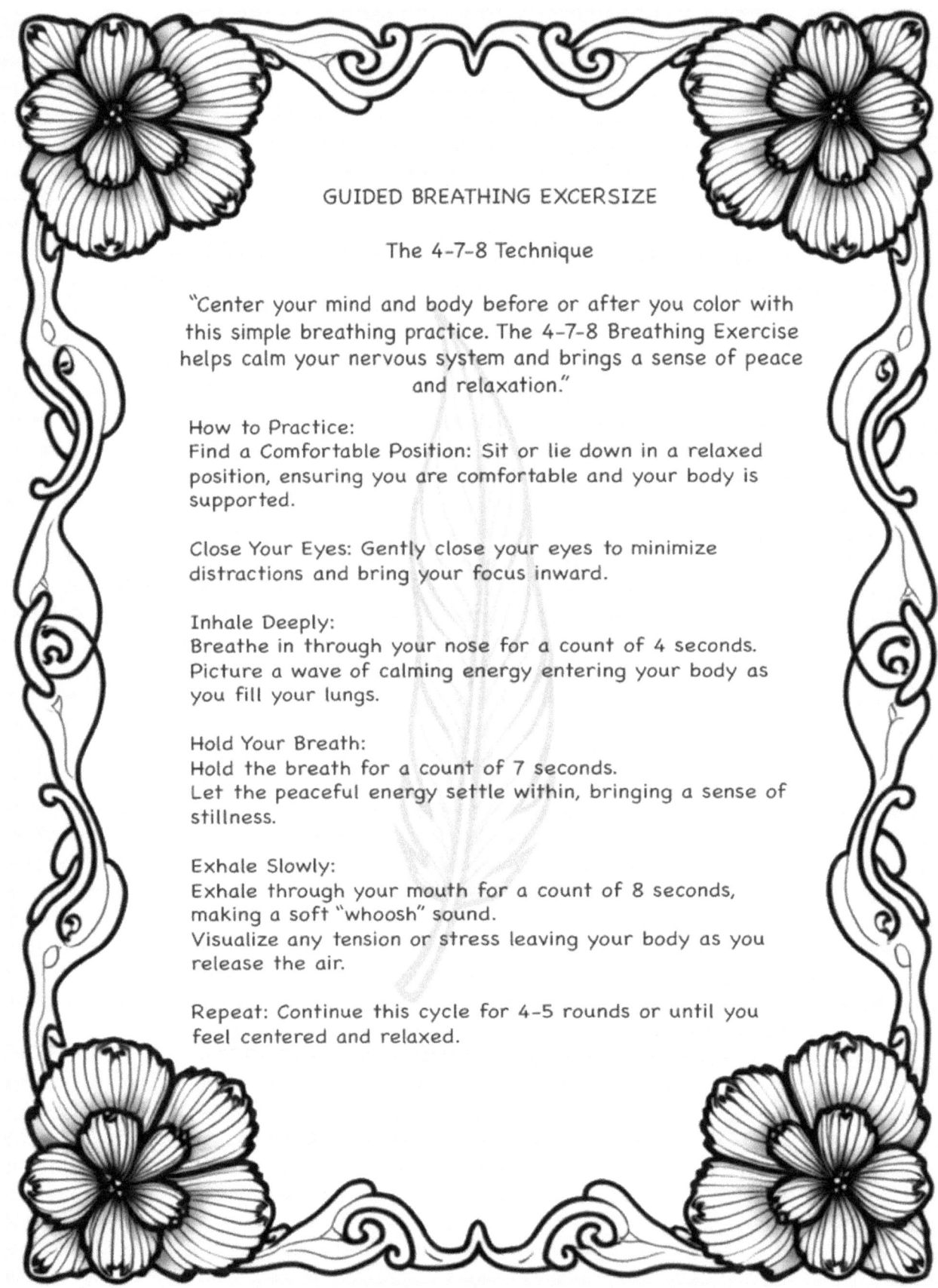

GUIDED BREATHING EXCERSIZE

The 4-7-8 Technique

"Center your mind and body before or after you color with this simple breathing practice. The 4-7-8 Breathing Exercise helps calm your nervous system and brings a sense of peace and relaxation."

How to Practice:
Find a Comfortable Position: Sit or lie down in a relaxed position, ensuring you are comfortable and your body is supported.

Close Your Eyes: Gently close your eyes to minimize distractions and bring your focus inward.

Inhale Deeply:
Breathe in through your nose for a count of 4 seconds.
Picture a wave of calming energy entering your body as you fill your lungs.

Hold Your Breath:
Hold the breath for a count of 7 seconds.
Let the peaceful energy settle within, bringing a sense of stillness.

Exhale Slowly:
Exhale through your mouth for a count of 8 seconds, making a soft "whoosh" sound.
Visualize any tension or stress leaving your body as you release the air.

Repeat: Continue this cycle for 4-5 rounds or until you feel centered and relaxed.

Mindful Check-In: Pause and Reflect

"Pause, take a deep breath, and check in with how you're feeling."

1. Close your eyes and breathe deeply. Notice the rhythm of your breath as it moves in and out.

2. Ask yourself: *How am I feeling right now?* Acknowledge your emotions without judgment, whether they're calm, joyful, or a bit unsettled.

3. Hold space for whatever comes up. Remind yourself that this moment is for you—let it be gentle and accepting.

Mindful Check-In: A Breath of Gratitude

"Take a deep breath and think of one thing you're grateful for today."

1. Inhale deeply, feeling your chest expand. As you exhale, let your shoulders drop and your body relax.

2. Think of one thing that has brought you joy or comfort today. It could be a person, a moment, or even a cozy blanket.

3. Hold onto that feeling of gratitude as you return to your coloring. Let it bring lightness to your heart.

Mindful Check-In: Relax Your Body

"Pause and scan your body. Where do you feel tension?"

1. Take a moment to pause and scan your body from head to toe.

2. Notice if you're holding any tension—in your jaw, shoulders, or hands. Take a breath and soften those areas.

3. Repeat this gentle body check-in throughout your coloring to stay relaxed and comfortable.

Mindful Check-In: Embrace the Present Moment

"Where is your mind right now? Bring it back to this moment."

1. If you find your thoughts wandering, gently guide them back to the present.

2. Focus on the here and now—feel your pencil in your hand, the colors in front of you, and the peaceful energy around you.

3. Remember: this moment is yours. Breathe, focus, and let yourself be fully here.

Mindful Check-In: Tune Into Your Senses

"Notice your surroundings. What do you hear, see, or feel?"

1. Take a moment to pause and look around. Observe the colors, light, and shapes in your space.

2. Listen carefully—what sounds do you hear? It might be soft music, distant voices, or the quiet hum of your environment.

3. Notice what you feel. Is it the warmth of a blanket, the texture of the paper, or the steady beat of your heart? Let this awareness ground you.

I am at ease, surrounded in of love and light

Mindful Check-In: Reflect on Your Creativity

"How does coloring make you feel right now?"

1. Take a brief pause and think about how this creative process is affecting your mood.

2. Are you feeling more relaxed, more joyful, or more focused? Simply observe without any pressure to change how you feel.

3. Carry this awareness into the rest of your session, allowing yourself to be fully immersed in the act of coloring.